Vinay Gupta edited the crowdsourced and crowdfunded *The Future We Deserve: 100 Essays About the Future* (2011). He coordinated the release of the Ethereum blockchain, and is CEO of Mattereum, the company creating digital identities for the world of physical goods. He has a background working in worst-case scenario planning and disaster mitigation, and is the inventor of the patent-free hexayurt, a sturdy, affordable, easy-to-build temporary shelter.

THE FUTURE OF STUFF

Vinay Gupta

unbound

First published in 2020

Unbound
Level 1, Devonshire House, One Mayfair Place, London W1J 8AJ
www.unbound.com
All rights reserved

With the kind permission of Tortoise Media

Text design by Ellipsis, Glasgow

A CIP record for this book is available from the British Library

ISBN 978-1-80018-012-3 (paperback)
ISBN 978-1-80018-014-7 (ebook)

Printed in Great Britain by CPI Group (UK)

1 3 5 7 9 8 6 4 2

To my guru, Bhavani Ma, who lived as a little old travelling nun with no home to rest her head, and constantly traversed America spreading light and love wherever she was invited to stay. She lived as an unknown, and these might be the only words in print about her, but the ripples she created will be felt across the world for centuries to come.

FOREWORD

Where and who do we want to be?

How might we get there?

What might happen if we stay on our current course?

This is one of the five books that, together, comprise the first set of FUTURES essays. Each short book in the set presents a beautifully written, original future vision by an accomplished writer and subject expert. Read individually, we hope these essays will inform, entertain and challenge. Together, we hope they will inspire readers to imagine what might lie ahead, to figure out how they might like the future to look, and think about how, collectively, we might make the transition from here to there, from now to then.

Over the life of the series we aim to publish a diverse range of voices, covering as broad a view of the future as possible. We ask our authors to write in a spirit of pragmatic hope, and with a commitment to map out potential future landscapes, highlighting both beauties and dangers. We are hugely proud of each of the essays individually, and of the set overall. We hope you get as much out of reading – and arguing with – them as we have from the process of getting them out into the world.

This first set of FUTURES would have been impossible to publish without the enthusiastic support of Tortoise Media, Unbound and the subscribers whose names you'll find listed at the back of each essay. Michael Kowalski, Tortoise's Head of Product, introduced co-founder Katie Vanneck-Smith to the idea, and she made it happen. Annabel Shepherd-Barron's unparalleled strategic capabilities kept the project steady and on course. Matthew d'Ancona offered superb editorial guidance with extraordinary kindness and generosity of spirit, and Jon Hill's designs for the book jackets are elegant perfection. Fiona Lensvelt, DeAndra Lupu and their colleagues at Unbound have proved wonderfully creative and flexible throughout.

This first set of FUTURES essays was commissioned in autumn 2019, in the midst of the Brexit saga, and edited in spring 2020, in lockdown, as Covid-19 changed everything. As we write, it looks unlikely that, by the time you read this, our lives will have settled into any kind of normal – old or new. Still, argument, wit and enlightened thought remain amongst our greatest strengths as a species, and even during an era as stressful and disorienting as the one we are experiencing, imagination, hope and compassion can help us mine greater reserves of resilience than we might expect. We hope these essays can, in a small way, help us find some light at the end of the tunnel.

Professor Max Saunders, Series Editor
Dr Lisa Gee, Programme Director and Editor
May 2020

THE FUTURE OF STUFF

SECTION ONE: JUSTICE AND DESIRE

SEEING UPSTREAM, SEEING DOWNSTREAM

There's no such thing as a car.

At least, there's no such stand-alone object called a car. If you think of the car as the 'figure' in the gestalt sense, the 'ground' on which the car stands is literally a road made just for the car. The car may have a tank of petrol in it, but there better be another tank of petrol right behind that one when it runs dry, or the car becomes a particularly expensive and impractical paperweight.

The fact that we think about and *price* the car as a stand-alone object, rather than as something embedded in a complex infrastructure, is how cars are able to do so much environmental and social damage, driving up house prices as parking competes with homes, destabilising the climate and threatening future food production with their noxious exhalations. In practice, we simply never price in the externalities of the car with the car: the roads, parking spaces, petrol stations and garages all divert resources from other causes, but car buyers do not pay for these things.

The car is like a cell in an invisible body we barely notice. This body can be perceived as Richard Dawkins's *extended phenotype*. The physical body of an animal, as defined by its DNA, is its *phenotype*. Dawkins argues that animals also have an *extended phenotype:* ants build ant hills, beavers build dams, humans create industrial society. Humans make cars, cars imply roads and petrol stations, but we do not see them as part of the car.

For everyday purposes, the perceived stand-alone 'carness' of the car is created by a narrowing of our attention away from the whole systems view. Because we usually think about the car and not the road, we lose the 'systemic embeddedness' which is actually crucial to the existence of the car. This tendency to see things but lose whole systems is a human perceptual limitation, like our blind spot. It is one aspect of what Gestalt psychologists call the Law of Prägnanz. The law states that the mind will perceive complex things in the simplest functional way: humans automatically cut complexity very early on in the perceptual system of the mind.

Gestalt psychology studies how we turn a complex, ever-shifting environment into coherent objects, including both concrete things like a pair of shoes, and abstract concepts like political parties. A critical part of this process is separating 'figure' (the thing) from 'ground' (everything else).

An artificial narrowing, a near-exclusive focus on the 'figure' of consumer goods to the total neglect of the 'ground' is at the heart of our problems reasoning about *stuff*. It affects us in all areas, from global warming to human rights to public health and product safety. At the heart of all of these problems is the *magical stuff illusion*: that stuff magically comes into existence when we buy it and magically leaves existence when we throw it away, much like the matter of the *Star Trek* 'Holodeck'. But real stuff is not like this; it is not conjured directly from the mind. In fact, all real stuff is the output of systems.

Seeing systemic embeddedness is central to our ability to reason about the future of stuff. The majority of the most revolutionary changes in the future of stuff will come from changes in the systems that produce the stuff. There is a gestalt between stuff and the systems which produce the stuff and, in this stuff/systems gestalt it is the production systems which shift first. New manufacturing technology or new financial arrangements enable the creation of new kinds of products. In manufacturing, the ground (tools) shifts before the figure (products).

The invisible networks of technologies and social practices which give *stuff* its value, its utility and its very existence are where all the innovation happens. The stuff comes along almost as an afterthought. Given new materials or new manufacturing technologies, designers will make a river of new things showcasing the wonders technology enables now.

There are two important classes of stuff we will not dig into very much in this work: infrastructure and appliances. Infrastructure is the pipes, wires, power stations, sewer pipes and aqueducts that connect our buildings to various service-provision architectures like power stations and water purification plants. Appliances, sometimes called white goods, are our refrigerators and washing machines, even our kitchen sinks. Although we could think of these things as stuff, and in some absolute sense they are, both infrastructure and appliances have complex interdependencies and dynamics of a kind which would warrant a book of their own to fully, formally explore. I spent a fair few years on these topics, under the banner *Simple Critical Infrastructure Maps*, and it is through that lens that I came to view so much of our world.

However, although we must gloss infrastructure and appliances, there is a third kind of special stuff which we will explore in some depth now.

THE MAGIC OF TOOLS

Tools are stuff that we use to make more, better stuff. The tools we use to run society firmly distinguish one age from another: this is, without a doubt, the laptop age giving over to the phone age. The laptop has been my tool of choice since 2001 when I bought the first 'square' iBook to hit the market: a white slab of productivity which was my workstation and which stayed that way, over several nearly identical machines, as the CD drive came and went and various ports appeared and disappeared, plastic gave way to metal, and ports finally vanished altogether, and that's what I'm writing on right now. I have some nostalgia for my old laptops: I will evoke a memory for certain readers by mentioning the X220 keyboard. Did that make you smile?

In any case, tools: a pen, and if it's special, your pen. Your computer, iPad, phone, tablet. Maybe your VR gear or gaming PC. Maybe your printer – do you still own a printer? Used to be essential – computers used to produce paper as their primary output (not email). In a kitchen, it's pans and the stove and the sink. Chefs, and their knives. Entire professions are identified mostly by their tools: anvils mean blacksmiths, as surely as stethoscopes signify doctors.

All these tools form a sort of landscape, a map. I start with a knife, a potato, a pan and some oil. There is a sequence of directions I can follow with these tools to make chips. The potatoes are food, a consumable, not really *stuff* in the sense we are interested in. The gas and cooker are infrastructure and an appliance, again not quite *stuff*. But everything else in that story is *tools* – the stuff we use to make

5

things. The tools you have expand the things you can cook or the things you can make.

Western civilisation – and, really, for the last hundred years, global civilisation – exists inside a framework that I christened AIAC, an acronym for *agro-industrial auto-catalysis*. Agro-industrial, because it is farms and factories which define our physical culture, and auto-catalysis because the more diverse our tools, the more sophisticated *stuff-making-stuff* we are using, the more we can accomplish when we combine and compose those capabilities.

This is the great mother system to which all other systems interconnect. It's the system which ensures you can buy steel bolts, a dollar a dozen, rather than having to take a tool and die set and carve the screw threads onto a piece of steel rod with a tap and die set yourself as you need it. AIAC means cheap food, cheap energy and cheap tools which in turn make more cheap food, cheap energy and cheap tools. Modern industrial civilisation is an ode to standardisation and the enormous profusion of complexity. It's like a jungle at the peak of its fertility, with an impossible number of plants and insects and other species all crammed in together passing nutrients back and forth. And, every year, that technical profusion grows and grows and grows, while (at the time of writing) that natural profusion dries, withers and burns away. The irony is savage.

Pretty much the only way to appreciate industrial civil-isation as an observer is to order a copy of the Grainger catalogue. I commend this exercise to the reader, particularly the younger reader: for a small fee, Grainger (the Amazon of industrial supplies) will ship you a catalogue where you could, with a sufficiently enthusiastic line of credit, order the basics of what you would need to equip a factory to build cars. It's a burly, multi-thousand-page paper brick which carefully curates most of the functional capacity of our cul-ture into a series of agonisingly narrow categories. You can just sit with it, hold it in your hands, randomly open a page and try and figure out what these things are for, who buys them, and, most important of all, *who makes them*.

This, then, is the magic of tools.

The tools that we have shape our ability to make things – a decent drill press makes holes in most steel a casually attainable goal. A 3D printer makes a wide range of mathe-matical surfaces easy to render as long as you only want them a few inches across and don't mind the rough wavy lines on the surface, the aliasing. What you can do depends on what you have.

There is a lyrical mysticism to our relationship with tools. My grandparents, on the Scottish side, were hand-and-eye people: a weaver and a carpenter. An inherited box of tools that my mother lugged around was a sacred object; it was *capi-tal* because she knew that, with it, a man could make a living.

Little did she realise when she bought me a toy computer in the late 1980s what kind of a tool she was bringing into the house. This is the essential experience I have of change: the older generation was hand tools for men, the younger generation was mind tools for everybody, and the generation in between was confused, the awkward stage between the two.

In our heads, we carry with us an invisible map, a *functional landscape* which surrounds our body like a third or fourth skin, our map of Dawkins's *extended phenotype*. If we are surrounded by trees and stones, and we have some know-how, we are also surrounded by axes, then log cabins. This invisible landscape of things which can be made into other things is often rendered in video games as a 'tech tree' – a landscape which players move over, in parallel with their similar movements over a physical map. The map tells you where you could go, and the tech tree tells you what your capabilities could be.

Our tools are an expression of the code in our DNA, exactly like our hair, fingernails, minds and internal organs. Perhaps humans really do make factories in the same way that beavers make dams. As we range over continents, we range over the technological landscape with these various bodies. Feet to walk, and hands to make, and minds to dream, each traversing its own kind of space: the *capability tensor* of our species, a multi-dimensional space which defines where we are and what we can become.

Here we have to consider the degree to which our DNA is software, and, as the program runs, it changes the world around us – an orchestrated dance of molecules self-organising into first bodies then tribes then nations, fire, farms, forges and factories as our major developmental stages. These systems are so deeply bound inside the human condition that nearly every culture has produced them, in one form or another. The human social structures which did not attend to this curve we tend to think of as being tribes: 'the hunter-gatherers'. The other cultures all followed a strange, interwoven trajectory – part biology, part trade, part culture – with much independent reinvention and repetition, towards the global technological society we enjoy today. To the limited extent that they survive and remain free, those hunter-gatherers are doing their own thing: they did not join us all out here on this burning branch we call civilisation. If global technological society crashes, their culture may comfortably outlast us by tens of thousands of years.

IT'S NOT THE CLOTHES THAT FIT YOU, IT'S YOU THAT FITS THE CLOTHES

Does anything you are currently wearing really fit *you*?

In most cases, the answer will be 'no'. If there does happen to be a fit, it is not because the clothes fit you, but rather that you fit the clothes. They were made for an abstract model, a dummy, and then you tried clothes on until you fit something. We like to think that we are the agents in this story, the protagonists, but actually (unlike craft tailoring) industrial mass production is not really about us. For a tailor, the first duty of the clothes is that they must fit, but in industrial capitalism the first duty of each mass-produced item is that it must *sell*. We exist as end points in a manufacturing process: as soon as the goods are sold, they are the buyer's property, and everything after that point is the buyer's problem.

Here, let's think about property rights. In most instances, a tailor will have a few rolls of cloth around. On the roll, if there's a decent amount of it, the cloth is worth a good chunk of what was paid for it: the cloth is a commodity which holds value. Once a customer is measured, and a fabric is selected, and the scissors come out, to all intents and purposes that cut cloth now belongs to the customer, because it has practically no value to anyone else. The cloth is now worth more to the customer as the makings of their suit than it was as yards upon a roll. Then assembly and a fitting: if all goes well, the physical custody of the clothes is passed to the customer, a payment is made and the job is done.

But there's a complex little dance in the middle, where an agreement is made, the cloth is cut, but the clothing not yet paid for. There is a little fuzzy blob of risk in there, carried by the tailor, that he'll do such a bad job the clothes won't be accepted by the customer – or the customer will suddenly become unable to pay for their clothes, or some other contingency. Once the cloth is cut it's useless to anybody except the intended wearer, but the tailor still bears the risk until a final payment is made. This little fuzzy ragged edge at the seam of the deal is where the risk in the deal concentrates. This may seem an odd example, but it's important to focus on the simplest and easiest questions about risk before we can see *risk* as the great next horizon in the future of stuff.

All manufacturing involves *risk*. The risk the stuff won't sell. The risk that the factory will burn down. The risk somebody will get hurt using the product, and you'll get sued.

Viewed through a risk lens, business exists in two basic forms: businesses that are tiny, and if something goes wrong, they die – small businesses, family businesses, startups – and behemoths so big and heavy that they can absorb a bunch of risk and just keep right on going. There are a lot of reasons that companies get big, but the simplest one is the question of reserves and amortisation of risks: a very big company can keep enough cash in hand that it can steamroller right over small mishaps by taking money out of the reserve, where a smaller company would go bankrupt. The large company knows how often things go wrong, and can calculate an optimal amount of reserve to cover the contingencies at hand. A small company can't afford the reserve: they just take their chances. This efficient management of contingencies is the simplest way of thinking about why big things are big, and it has broad consequences.

It's not always a specific manufacturing economy of scale which makes the big more profitable than the small: it's the very nature of risk. In an ever-faster changing world, we see a profusion of tiny little companies exploiting micro-niches and trying to find the ever-elusive product–market fit, but also the creation of enormous platforms which dominate entire sectors of life like Amazon, Google, Facebook, Walmart, Airbnb, Microsoft and Uber. Those behemoths do things in ways that suit them, not that necessarily us, their customers.

It's not the clothes that fit you, it's you that fits the clothes.

A BRAND IS A THING SEARED INTO THE SIDE OF A COW

Things reflect the organisations which make them. Brands sell this to us: the Apple temple is intended to produce things which bring technology into the domain of the secular sacred. There are certainly Apple devices which have changed human history: the original iPod is, I think, a good candidate for the 'Gutenberg press' of music going digital, a trend with massive long-term cultural impacts. The reality that Apple wishes to create is that of a sort of Techno-Zen shrine, with ascended master Steve Jobs inspiring customers to greater creativity and self-actualisation. This story, however, is no more real than the dream-world stuff that advertisements speak of, which winks into existence at desire and vanishes at disgust. The sacred object is a thin veil that may exist in a few design departments and at the board level of Apple. But behind the scenes Apple is still all heavy truck fleets and Chinese factory workers in surgical masks spending their entire work lives polishing bits of glass before the products are packed into the sea containers. All brands are like this: a numinous veil drawn over a basically standard, efficient manufacturing operation with different degrees of ugliness and decrepitude forced into the corners.

This structure does not exist by chance. Factories are horrible. Even nice factories are kind of horrible, but bad factories are really horrible. All factories were bad factories in the early days of industrialisation. Belts drove spindles on machines, and a careless hem could get caught in the spindle or the belt, wind you up in the works and kill you in the blink of an eye. It wasn't like shearing sheep or swinging a scythe: people could get killed or maimed doing it, and frequently did. Industrial accidents, pollution, exposure to toxic chemicals. Those 'dark satanic mills' of the early industrial revolution were indeed hells. Factories in countries without strong labour unions and health and safety regulations tend towards the hellish to this day. This pattern – where along the supply chain, gross matter is transmuted into the wonder of consumer products – is older than the factory. It goes back at least as far as feudalism. Here, in Britain, I like to think of it as the class divide embodied in our very language: 'beef' on the plate from the French *boeuf*, but 'cow' in the field, from the Anglo-Saxon *cū*. The cooked dish is identified using the language of the masters, but the animal on the hoof is named in the language of the farmers.

Unconsciously a person asks: do I have enough money, enough status in this situation, to have somebody draw the veil over how this was made to create the beautiful illusion of consumer products which appear *as if by magic* and disappear in exactly the same way when I am done with them, or do I have to deal with this all myself? Do I hire somebody, or is this DIY? Are we closer to the manufacturers who witness stuff being made as underpaid, downtrodden workers, maybe even children, make the product on a factory line, or are we the consumers for whom a web of enchantment is woven by advertising, temporarily patching the hole in our soul with cheap credit? From which vantage point do we see the stuff? *On which side of the retail counter do we stand?*

Stuff exists on a timeline: its manufacturing and its sale, its use by the consumer and its disposal. At every stage, the paying customer is separated from the inconvenient truth – be it blood diamonds, factory workers being ground down, or vast seas of rotting landfill. Consumerism has learned that it is more profitable to *lie to us about our stuff*, and about the consequences of buying our stuff. We are so well served by these lies that we have come to cherish and sacralise them – the Mall and Luxury are now as archetypal as the watering hole and gold itself these days – an entire fantasy world wrapped around the rich, much as theme parks enfold children.

But everything is temporary, even structural lies that outlast empires are eventually killed by the truth. Ours is a little bubble in history, a moment in time when the distance goods travel is further than the distance news about how those goods are made travels: a mismatch between the power of advertising and the power of auditing, if you will.

The gaps in history where lies overpower truth will close in time, just as prices being arbitraged between markets will eventually equalise. Buyers and sellers will meet, not only on the price that the goods are to be sold at, but with an agreed narrative about where the goods came from, how they were made and where they are going at the end of their utility. Because consumers do not only want *stuff* these days, they are starting to want the truth about their *stuff*. The climate crisis puts immense moral pressure on all of us to clean up our lifestyles. That trend towards transparent capitalism is only fully visible among status-driven luxury consumers today, but it will inevitably spread as a new horizon for social competition, as people want to separate themselves from the evils of the world by building enclaves of sustainable, fair trade commerce.

Nobody wants to be the only kid in class wearing slave-labour jeans. Social pressure will move standards far faster than legislation, in many arenas.

THE AGE OF WILFUL IGNORANCE IS AT AN END

Things have been really bad for a really long time.

You can look in almost any direction in the past, or things left over from the past, and see something so horrible the modern mind recoils just from looking at it. Roman laws on child prostitution, or the reports on the UN personnel abusing their immunity to prosecution. How foie gras is made. The feet of ballet dancers. So many of our cultural institutions come from a barbaric age when doctors did not wash their hands, women died all the time in childbirth and princes did what they damn well liked and nobody was allowed to say 'boo' (never mind 'lawsuit'). The ages before us were lawless, ignorant, dangerous and violent, often all at the same time.

During those times, just to get through the day meant doing things very few of us would be physically ready, psychologically able or morally willing to do today. It takes a special mindset to raise animals, see them every day, give them names, pat them on the head, and then, at the end of the year, slaughter and eat them. We still have plenty of people who do it, but far fewer as a percentage of our population than was once the case. Feudal lords may have got enough to eat most of the time, but they sat in the middle of a sea of envy and hatred, and could be forced to fight in wars on the words of one guy who inherited the right to tell them what to do, just as they inherited the land they rented out to the local vassals. The past was basically terrible.

It had its points, but it was basically terrible.

Colonialism is essentially the export of feudalism around the world, as well as reviving or inventing several new cruelties along the way. None of us were alive when that horrible process began, yet nearly all of us indirectly benefit from it today: Indian gold built the Victorian sewers and the other public infrastructure that hauled London out of squalor. This often seems like it is in the past but just as with ballet, the barbaric practices of the past continue to break toes now, because we keep the barbaric past alive – *even though we would simply never countenance these practices if they were invented today*. We got used to the pretty bits and that familiarity prevented us from seeing things clearly: come for the ballet, stay for the broken toes.

The real problem with our stuff is how much of it is produced by slaves, by child labour, by clear-cutting rainforests, shooting elephants, skinning mink alive and 400 other activities we would completely recoil at doing ourselves, and *frankly* are a bit sick of people doing on our behalf. Nobody is suggesting we actually *ban* ballet, but there sort of comes a point where people look at the damage done from standing on your toes all day, or smashing your head into the helmet of some other college student to the point of getting brain damage, and we basically say *enough!* This is exactly where we are with trade: we have collectively had enough of the barbarity, and now we need a way for it to end. As I used to say when discussing the 2008 financial collapse, 'Collapse means living in the same conditions as the people who grow your coffee.'

The barbaric past dies only when we get uncomfortable enough with the evil being done by the customs of the past that we decide that, actually, we are not sending our kids to ballet school unless they will not be doing pointe, and our sons are doing basketball not football until something is *done* about the traumatic brain injuries.

We cannot help that our lives are deeply, deeply embedded in the barbaric practices of the past, any more than we can help that once in a blue moon somebody winds up ordering the foie gras and we guiltily pinch a bite. Nobody's morality is absolute; we are all fish in water arguing who is the wetter.

But, right now, we are at a staggeringly high peak in the history of humans communicating with each other, at the same time as nearly everything we buy (except maybe the occasional fair trade organic raisin) contains a history of brutal oppression at some level, somewhere in its history. Even if your car runs on oil from Norway, that oil is cheap because of the oil coming out of the Middle East and fracking. It's all an enormous moral tangle and if only a single consumer changes their mind, it is too expensive and complex to live the entirely moral life.

No lesser a light than Mahatma Gandhi encountered this problem. Gandhi wore his iconic uniform consisting of a shawl and shorts made of khadi to make it clear to his followers that it was better to wear a small amount of the ethically manufactured (but expensive) hand-woven Indian fabric than to wear a full suit of clothes made by the oppressive machinery of the British Empire – that is to say, the looms that were being operated in Scotland by my grandmother at the time of Gandhi's campaigns. Gandhi was making the point that nobody is too poor to wear ethically produced things: if you have to make do with less, because your morality insists on fair trade, you are not without honour. This Gandhian principle alone is half the answer to the world's problems, if only people would act en masse as they did in Gandhi's time.

The destructive ignorance of the past is being replaced with a witheringly harsh, scouring transparency. The same new integrated cross-organisation technology platforms that we need for maximum industrial and financial efficiency also lay the foundation for transparency up and down the supply chain, revealing unfair labour practices and environmental crimes at the same time as they identify waste and inefficiency. In the future there will be no place to hide the oppression.

Take food safety as an example. If there is a recall of, say, a contaminated salad product, the most efficient recall is one which figures out exactly where the contagion originated. Perhaps all the salads contained lettuce from the same farm in Sonoma. So now only those packages are recalled. The next step is to identify and correct what went wrong in Sonoma and guarantee that it will never cause an expensive recall again. To get the efficient outcome requires transparency. That transparency extends right down to 'our migrant workers did not have proper sanitation facilities, and that is how this salad became contaminated'. Getting to root causes and fixing expensive problems requires transparency. The alternative is a constant stream of produce recalls and lawsuits. These liabilities spread up the supply chain, and so there is constant pressure for transparency from both retailers and customers.

This is not a new approach: *transparency is profitable*. In fact, transparency is the only path to quality in manufacturing. This has been well known in industrial manufacturing since the post-Second World War period. A US quality control expert called W. Edwards Deming laid the foundation for modern electronics manufacturing in Japan when he transformed organisational culture around values like transparency and cooperation to get the incredible clarity required to perfect complex manufacturing processes.

In the age of the Internet, however, this kind of transparency takes on an entirely different aspect. Labour struggles continue and organise online. The people making the goods can see on Instagram the lifestyles of the people using the things they made. Slowly it becomes harder and harder to maintain the structural inequalities left behind by colonialism, particularly as former colonies rise to their feet as global powers. The push and pull here is a direct continuation of the struggles of labour unions during the industrial period, but now rendered as global politics. But let us not forget that we are all the beneficiaries of victories in previous rounds of this fight. Our forty-hour work weeks and two-day weekends all came from the struggle of factory workers and miners and farmers, all over the world, every day, as they fought and still fight, right now, for better wages and workplace protections.

As we forced those above us to make room at the table in the past, so we must make room at the table now, until for everyone, there is bread.

SUCH STUFF AS DREAMS ARE MADE OF

Looking at the struggle of workers locates our story squarely inside the logic of industrial mass production inside of market capitalism. Pretty much any discussion of the future of 'stuff' is going to start inside that conceptual frame, because that's where the stuff is made, but it is too limited on its own.

Now we have to break that frame. We need a god's eye perspective. One more illusion must be peeled away before we can construct a durable watchtower from which to view the future.

Mass production, or even craft production, is not where the *stuff* actually came from. In an absolute sense the atoms came from the Big Bang, and stellar nucleosynthesis making heavy atoms like gold inside supernovae, and the cosmic processes which brought Earth into being, with all its metals, ores and stone, and the various waves of geology and biology that made our raw materials like coal and oil, and contemporary biological processes that give us wood, cotton, all of our food except maybe salt, and so on. Apart from a few things made in nuclear reactors, like the sources inside X-ray machines, every atom was made by impossibly ancient processes which are completely outside our control, processes that we even now do not fully understand.

It used to be that we had religious or spiritual myths to explain where the *stuff* came from. Gods of rivers, gods of the earth, myths about fornicating titans and what have you. Now we have reasonably accurate models – as far as they go. For every kind of atom, we can track back to roughly what kind of nuclear reactions happened in roughly what kinds of stars back more or less to the Big Bang. At the big physics labs we can tear the atoms apart into quarks and gluons, and point at neutrinos by watching them make flashes of light as they interact with atoms in enormous dark underground lakes of dry-cleaning fluid surrounded by impossibly sensitive detectors. But why these fundamental particles and not others; why these fundamental forces? There is very little in the way of coherent science when we take a step past there: we have neither the experimental equipment nor the theoretical frameworks to take us further. These are the rules of the game, and we play inside them as we will. Future generations will expand that understanding, but we may never solve it.

In a very real sense, nobody ever made anything.

People rearrange pieces which already exist, in much the same way that kids make things from Lego, but do not themselves manufacture the Lego bricks. That's our entire economy, and all of our manufacturing processes: rearranging things that literally just fell from the sky. And most of our art, except perhaps stories. And life itself is made of this *stuff* in forms which draw more energy from the environment than they need to survive, for a while, and then this life duplicates itself, sometimes in partnership with mates, into forms ever so slightly different from the forms which went before. Iterated over a billion years, a mysterious first replicator – a thing without a face, without a name, one tiny event away from being inanimate matter – this thing lit a fire which still burns today, one billion years later. We are that fire, and that fire is us.

But, outside of a few nuclear reactors making isotopes for industrial reasons, the atoms and the fundamental forces are exactly where the clockwork machinery of physics put them. There is a little island of life here on earth where things work a little differently, but where matter self-organises into self-replicating things which become people who write books like this, and people who read them, but for the most part *stuff just is*.

So what we are really tracking here, as we think about the future of stuff, is *the future of material culture*: what you would see in future museums in glass cases, eternal and unchanging. The way people make patterns in the *stuff* is what changes. Our stuff is *patterns plus atoms* for the most part. And the patterns we make are 100% embodied material culture, from clothes to nuclear reactors. Everything is embedded.

In fact, what is happening when we *make stuff* is that we are binding cultural information – science, engineering, craft, technology and art – to rearrange these fixed atoms in front of us into forms which are more pleasing to our hand, our eye and even our deepest psychological needs. This mixing of matter and information is as old as life itself: in fact, it *is life itself*. DNA is the first physical manifestation of information, and, if you want to be absolutist about it, information is life. A persistent pattern in the entropic heat and noise of the universe is literally the difference between being alive and dead.

We lay our hands on the raw matter that fell from the skies, and we use it to carry information. The tools of the hunt and the field carry our DNA by helping us survive and reproduce, just as oil paint carries our dreams. Biology and culture, winding around each other down through time for millions of years.

What makes the *stuff* important to us is its ability to modulate and carry the *signal*. And the signal?

The signal is *life itself*.

Life is replicating information.

INSTINCT AND DESIRE: *I WANT THAT!*

Desire is the most primal interaction we have with our environment, and therefore our stuff. Back at the start, before life was people, our ancestors flowed along chemical gradients towards life and light, towards sustenance and opportunity. What those creatures wanted was good for life, because only the ones who felt desire for what was good for them survived. And so life exists, and life goes on.

Now compare this to our modern experience. Cunning minds on the other side of the world guess what we want for a living, and commit the kind of resources which could have built a university campus to building factories and designs for that consumer product they imagine we want. I'm writing this book on just such a device: silicon and aluminium, the bitten apple and, below it in the operating system, a dull reflection of Richard Stallman's dreams.

You may not have heard of Richard Stallman. It is my considered opinion that he will be remembered far longer than Gandhi, and I'm quite a fan of Gandhi. Stallman is an American computer programmer, and the elder statesman/embarrassing uncle of the Free Software movement. I cannot explain in detail Stallman's philosophical struggle, but we can talk about what came from it: hundreds of billions of dollars of assets, in the form of software and information repositories including Wikipedia, which are available without any payment, and with *legally guaranteed* rights for users, all over the world. Linux, Android and the Macintosh OS itself are all built on Free Software, or its dilution, Open Source. This movement is one of the most successful examples of mass collaboration in human history. However, Stallman is a personal hero really only to those who write software for a living: an industry-specific hero. But the fundamental reason that anything is Free on the Internet is Richard Stallman. Stallman figured out that our future *cognitive and political freedom* depended on our ability to control the software that manages our lives. That process has been partially successful: many high-quality zero-cost applications and operating systems which respect the rights of their users now exist, even as behemoths like Facebook, Amazon and Google have tried to claw back control of user data. The struggle continues, and the tactics change with each new generation of technology.

All these computer systems are packed with information, the spectacular information density of the microprocessor, and the vast information system that manages to keep this document entirely safe as I type it, every character immediately backed up on the Internet's largest machine, the great cluster in which all our email is stored, which gives us *search*. The pattern of information is so powerful, the capability is so powerful, that most of us use it every single day with as little thought as we give the workings of our socks. And yet, to see what makes that machine work is to see a scale so far beyond the human, the pastoral, our ancestral villages. A single global machine which knows and tells, that sings and gives us stories, that we would miss every day more than *fire*. We are a long way from home, humans. We are far, far from our roots.

But is the fundamental impulse that we feel when we see beautiful stuff, this *I want that!*, any different from those early single-celled organisms climbing up the chemical gradient towards life? Is the thing that makes me want things different from the thing which made them want things?

Well, we're all just made of cells, right? And cells want stuff that makes them happy, and that started out as sunlight to make sugars, and wound up with Coach handbags. We are just assemblages of those tiny primal life shapes, those cells, in the same way that we are just assemblages of atoms and forces.

It's all bedrocked on this same fundamental desire. To life!

Think about the last thing you bought because you just wanted it. The last thing that had that immediate, primal sense of *desire*. This is beautiful, this is good, this is right, this belongs with me, this should belong to me, this must be mine. Sunlight to make sugar, that desire filtered by the aeons, into this.

Now, here's the question: go back 50,000 years. Could your ancestors even recognise what this thing that you want *is*?! I got a pretty cool high-tech blanket when I was in America just before the coronavirus hit. I bet my ancestors could figure out what that is for. But the next thing I bought after that, a flexible tripod, is not something a cave-dweller could relate to at all, except as a lousy club.

So somehow we have spun up an enormous edifice which takes these basic chemical imperatives to preserve and duplicate information in genes, and it has given rise to *abstract needs* and infinitely complex culture. We are running up some strange exponential ramp, but to where, and why?

Cells like energy. Sugar is energy. DNA wants to replicate, because the DNA which didn't want to replicate is not here too much any more, and DNA needs energy to replicate. Desire is biology, and shopping is metabolism. But somewhere here we have created a machine, a vast apparatus, which takes these relatively simple desires and makes Fabergé eggs.

What's going on? This isn't a neutral question in an easy

time to be alive. This virus we call consumerism is wrecking our world by threatening those fundamental biological processes. Consumerism in no way drives life or creates life, but in fact poisons our lives and the planet itself: it's almost like a cultural cancer or an auto-immune disorder. All these things we make which do not give life or give satisfaction to life, the things which clutter and consume us as much as we consume them: how did we wind up surrounded by these parasites?

Someone sold us to them, in the act of selling them to us.

And it is not that I am against things or beauty, but if we are to think about the future of stuff, we must have a wizard's eye for the present. Nobody is going to tell us how the cage we are in was constructed, unless they too wish to escape.

I want that, but, really, *did I want **this**?* The world has become cluttered with things which are neither useful nor beautiful, and we don't seem able to stop buying them. What junk food does to bodies this new consumerism does to hearts, minds, souls and wallets. In a sense, modern overconsumption is as evil as tobacco: an addiction with huge life-destroying externalities like credit card debt. This giant information machine on which I type this message to you, it also watches me type and tries to sell me the things that I write about! It's the price I pay for instant backup to the cloud of every character as I write it. It would literally take a cosmic event for me to lose one character of this text. 'Life is information' and, well... what is more appealing to the mind than *the backup*? Information which will never be lost, permanence, eternal truth, security against forgetting: information loves to be durable. Risk management penetrates every layer of our minds.

And yet, the externalities of feeding this addiction we all have to stuff are horrendous. That addiction fills the landfills and sweatshops of the world every single day, making things we do not *really* want or need, and crowding out the real needs in imagined ones on a truly epic scale. Right now, I'm writing at the start of the 2020 coronavirus epidemic.

I can walk across the street to the Tottenham Hale Retail Park and find 20,000 shirts and jackets, and junk food in every possible permutation. But not a single face mask.

Fake needs and real needs are competing for space in those stores, and in our minds, and the confusion between the two is as toxic as crude oil.

REIFICATION OF SYMBOLS

Pooh Bear wants *honey*. We'll forget, for the moment, the struggle of the worker bees, seen only as little black dots around his honey-addled head. Focus on the symbol: what Pooh Bear *wants*, this primal seed of desire. The roly-poly little fellow wants honey! It is inborn: *Pooh is a Bear, and Bears want Honey!*

We, of course, see *Pooh's Honey* as a symbol, because we are not storybook bears, but humans. And if there is one thing humans love it is symbols, perhaps as much as bears love honey. To us, Pooh's life is a story about desire, about avarice, about foolishness (at times), and always, of course, about friendship. But a version of Pooh Bear that does not want honey is *barely Pooh Bear*. Desire defines him.

We all have our *Honey*. It is apparently the nature of life to want things. Plants want sun, because sun is sugar, and sugar is energy, and energy is needed to store and duplicate information. The bees store the honey to *live*! To a bee, honey is *liquid summer*, the light and heat of the long days, stored up in the hive away from the coldness of winter and the night. So Pooh Bear desires a thing which is precious indeed!

But where in this story does the $35,000 handbag emerge as a thing that a person looks at and says, *I want that!* How did our primal, metaphysical need to store and replicate information – the core function which makes us alive – become so damn *abstracted*?

The truth is, nobody wants a handbag that expensive to carry their keys, lipstick and Glock 42. What people want is to be desired, to be respected, to show they have attained a social standing in which the biological needs of their distant descendants are likely to be met – to show, in short, that they have won the biological game so completely that they can

31

spend the labour of a year for an ordinary worker to make things with no immediate survival value. The tail of the peacock is there to show potential mates that the peacock is alert, agile and aggressive enough to manage in the world with so much of its energy manifested as beauty, *as wonder*, as, indeed, *biological art*. The individual peacock may not consciously make art in the same way a person does, but the peacock *genes* make art as surely as Michelangelo.

The $35,000 handbag is a staff of office.

I can't tell you the purposes of such instruments – I understand the lives of the women (and the few men) that wield such instruments about as well as I understand the lives of bees. But I can say this: the handbag says unambiguously, 'I can afford this,' and that opens up a lot of doors! In an expensive venue, it says, 'I am a guest and a customer,' not a rubbernecking lowlife to be hustled out of the store. In some cultures it says, 'You will treat me well, or there will be real consequences.' And *everywhere* it says, 'I don't need you for your money, *Honey*.'

Wealth is to humans what honey is to bees – *liquid summer* – although we seem to have become weirdly addicted to the stuff. Can you imagine bees with swimming pools full of honey, enormous reserves the size of beaver dams? That does not seem to be the way bees think. Why is it the way we think? Compare the collectors of classic cars against the nomads of Mongolia, or ask how much yacht is enough yacht?

It's all stored life. It's all *capital*. The tears of the sun, gold. One principle, one story, one symbol – at the heart of things, hot, energetic, fiery, valuable, filled with potential. *Liquid summer*. The light of the sun!

It's all in pursuit of life, but the cultural feedback loops of our strange game of civilisations have left our poor ape brains addled as people and machines teach us to want what we don't need, because, where we are now, wanting what we don't need is part of the game that gets us to the higher strata of society.

When I went from academia to the periphery of the City of London, I bought a watch. Nothing fancy, and nothing new. I'm Scottish working class, albeit a Hindu hybrid with strong monastic tendencies. I was not going for the Rolex: that's a car on your wrist.

But once I had that watch, and a pair of shoes and a suit to match, and lost the beard and a few other things, something changed. Suddenly I was a person of the City. I was somebody who had done something worthy of notice before, but I was not noticed because I did not have the trappings. The symbols of the office were required before I could be recognised as a very junior part of the City of London scene.

Symbols are socially real. In a world with strict environmental limits, this fact is our nemesis. Our peacock tails reach to every nook and cranny of the earth, making the display.

SECTION TWO: DESIRE AND DESTINY

If we have a role in the future as human beings, we must learn to *desire* in a way which is compatible with the story of our species continuing far into the future. If we cannot want what is biologically good for us, maybe robots will 'read' this book as they assimilate the human cultural archives on their way to the stars.

Right now we do not have that framework. In fact, we are heavily restricted in our ability to see our way to a biologically sustainable future because of overconsumption. It's that simple: we want the wrong things and we satisfy those desires at the cost of our core biological agendas around staying alive and keeping our genes in the world after us (either directly or not). How are we to survive and prosper through this? How are we to overcome the limits that evolution has left us, in willpower, in perspicacity, in cognition, fundamentally in *mastery*? How are we to get on top of this avalanche of problems unleashed by building the industrial society which feeds us all (well, many of us) and could feed the rest, if we could just organise it a little better?

I have an answer: we are going to automate morality.

MACHINES THAT WORK FOR US VERSUS MACHINES THAT WORK ON US

Machines made this mess. Very literally, industrial mass production made this mess: we can make more than we need, and we take more than we need, and the result is chaos and biological damage to our bodies and to the world. Consider our worst offender, the car. The car hasn't actually had to be made of two tons of steel for safety reasons for several decades, but we are trapped by the slowness with which regulation catches up with new technology. We massively overbuild heavy steel cars because using modern lightweight materials is a regulatory nightmare. But while this situation continues, every mile driven makes it less likely that your great grandkids will ever see grass.

What kind of crazy monkey gets caught in such a trap?

The answer is very simple: a monkey ruled by bad machines, not by people. To all intents and purposes *the things are in charge of us*. This fear is manifested in popular culture as the fear of artificial intelligence, the feeling that in some way the robots of the mind are going to overwhelm us and destroy our ability to determine our own destiny. The argument is often made that corporations and governments are actually examples of such artificial intelligences, but with individual human beings as the computing nodes on which these metastable systems impose their preternatural wills on reality. In short, some people see a corporation as a machine made of people, operating software which is made of corporate law, contracts and abstract principles like 'shareholder interests'.

A government, or a nation state, or a religion, is so far divorced from the lifespan of a single human and that human's needs that they are basically a force of 'nature' if not actually a machine. These cultural heritage patterns have strength and stability so far beyond human will and human purpose that they may as well be rivers, snaking their way through time, carrying us all with them and, occasionally, flooding into wars and destroying everything around them.

How, then, are we to take back control of this situation?

The answer is simple: we are going to make machines that work *for the best in us* rather than *working on the worst of us*.

Go back to advertising for just a minute. Beer, like most things being mainly advertised to men, is usually advertised by associating it with conventionally attractive women. And so are cars, and sports gear, and most other things which are being sold to men. It's either attractive women, high social status among other men, or huge wide-open vistas of unoccupied nature – land. The biological message is clear: you'll have lots of kids, people will respect you and your many kids will populate the landscape long after you are gone. Life is good, we've got all that we need and everybody thinks you are great! I can't pretend to fully understand how products are sold to women, but it seems to involve a lot of seriously overdressed, really skinny tall girls laughing while they eat salad in expensive-looking venues.

Who wouldn't want such lives? But I don't think there's a product I can buy which will deliver them to you or me. The advertisement simply attempts to make a false association between that which is biologically successful and that which is sold. A very simple play is being made to build a false association between some *stuff* and basic biological drives, and this kind of adversarial programming of humans is increasingly being done with artificial intelligence techniques: Internet advertising is A/B-tested, multiple versions of the advertisements shown to different demographic clusters extracted using pervasive monitoring, processed using fabulous algorithms, until the adverts with the highest financial return become those we see all around us. You buy nappies, you're going to see kids' stuff on every web page you visit which has advertising on it for the next six months.

But these things also try to crawl inside your soul.

These AIs are being trained to do whatever is most profitable: to condition you into buying things you do not really want or need, simply because it happens to be profitable. There is no notion of meaning, of purpose, of semantics in these algorithms: they are the dumbest form of predatory desire, given cunning but no wit. What chance does an ordinary – or even an extraordinary – human being have against pervasive monitoring and vast statistical shaping of their needs, wants, desires and behaviour by an all-pervasive amoral monitoring network? Who can remain free under such pressure?

If we did this to animals, we would call it training. We are being trained to jump through arbitrary consumption hoops with the promise of future treats, and those future treats only need to be delivered long enough for the habits to be ingrained.

We must send a machine to fight this machine.

WHAT CAN DEFEND US FROM IMAGINARY NEEDS?

The most subversive thing we can do is to know what is good for us.

This applies to everything: health, mental wellbeing, clothes, work, art, music – to have your own taste and knowledge of your own needs is revolutionary in a society which thrives on mass production coupled to targeted advertising. And, while many individuals may converge on a love of the same thing, Vampire Weekend or Placebo or Bruno Mars or whatever, they all like it for their own reasons, in their own way. Cells love sugar, but infinite diversity in infinite combinations explosively evolves from that basic need, and we should not forget this.

So how do we know what is good for us, and, indeed, good for the people around us, our potential or actual descendants, and for the world and life itself? How, in short, do we know what is *moral* in the most absolute frame of reference we can find?

We construct machines to know on our behalf, and they sort this mess out for us.

A few years ago, there was a great debate on the use of plastic bags in stores. Plastic bags were evil but, on later analysis, paper bags were evil, too, or so the debate went. The debates were inconclusive, and on weak evidence governments started to slap a tiny minimum price on plastic bags, slashing use. But was it paper or plastic? Or should we have gone delivery, and skipped going to the store at all? What precisely was the lean, green, environmentally efficient choice here? Is a million people each zipping around carrying their own groceries really the smart way of doing this?

We had no social *machinery* to find out. Governments basically made the decision on a whim, and academic study was inconclusive. The effects were not large in any case, and the entire issue kind of slid past us.

Something similar happened four decades ago with recycling. Recycling is, generally speaking, roughly environmentally neutral - it doesn't help the environment very much, if at all. There are some cases where it's great – steel and aluminium, say – but most of the time pulling apart products which were never intended to be recycled is basically not worth doing in either environmental or economic terms. It just takes too much time and energy. A lot of it is done by children who work on garbage heaps in horrendously poor places. The pictures are depressing. It's not good. It's not even close to okay. However, if we had done an accurate net assessment of environmental strategies in the 1970s *everything would have been focused on energy efficiency* – immediate financial rewards align with outstanding environmental impact reductions. It's the clear, clear win of all the things we can do. Energy efficiency is mostly builders doing more skilful jobs, architects thinking about the long-term use of buildings and appliance designers watching what goes into their machines, not just what comes out. It's clean work, to use less energy. No children living on garbage dumps are required.

For the first time in my life I live in a decently insulated house with carbon-neutral heating (via a district heating system that runs on wood chips). Environmental efficiency is *great*: it's a warm house with low bills. What's not to love? Compare this to volunteers at conferences rummaging through garbage bags making sure everything goes into the right one. One of these things is part of the future, the other is simply bad information and misaligned incentives resulting in people being saddled with inconvenient, dirty, meaningless tasks. And pity the kids who live on the garbage dumps.

So the decisions we make culturally about what is important stick for decades, even when there is plenty of evidence to the contrary. People get stuck on bad ideas about how to help the world.

Energy efficiency has been the biggest possible environmental win for decades, and we just could not turn the cultural ship towards this goal. How can we correct that, not just for energy efficiency, but for *everything*?

What I want is a machine to help me make decisions in a moral way. Making morally correct decisions is too hard for individuals when supply chains or science are involved. It is too difficult and time-consuming to correlate all the relevant information and be confident we have come to the right conclusions. There should be a machine that aggregates all the information about the environmental and social impact of our purchases to steer us towards the right choices. Of course, in areas that require complex moral reasoning, this is impossible with today's technology. But when it comes to buying *stuff*, figuring out the morally right thing to do comes down to impact analysis. A machine only has to be able to compare the impacts of the things I might buy, and present me with the least damaging option. In this domain, the morally right answer is the one with lowest environmental and social impact – it's not an unbounded moral problem with ambiguous choices. Under these simplified conditions, a machine can choose what does least harm and most good.

Computers do similar kinds of decision making for us all the time. GPS maps on phones are indispensable because they identify the shortest route between two points. Flight search engines get you the lowest cost flight, hotel room or rental car. There is no fundamental reason I should not be able to use a machine to find the least socially and environmentally damaging clothes, phone or laptop.

At an even simpler level, why can't shopping sites like Amazon or eBay or Ocado just give me the option to block products made in horrible ways? *Never attempt to sell me something that would make me puke if I knew the whole story, okay?*

Charities, academics, governments, activists, even customers collectively have all parts of the information needed to build these decision-making tools, in much the same way that groups like Ordnance Survey and many different satellite mapping and drone survey companies all had pieces of the data needed to create modern digital maps. Society just had to build the right machines to integrate all these systems together to get the breakthrough in capabilities that we enjoy every day.

I use the term machine in the broadest sense. What got us digital maps in the long run involved almost every sector of society: government-funded GPS systems, decades of university research, start-up companies, tech behemoths, hardware manufacturers and many actors had to come together to build these cutting-edge capabilities into our everyday lives.

When morality was defined by religion, it was largely based on sexual morality and maybe a bit of instruction about taking care of the very poor. Morality was defined by received wisdom, and all the machinery to implement morality was social. Then over time the role of managing hard limits on morality largely passed to the state, as it took over from religions as the primary maker of law. The state eventually outsourced most of the hard analysis about the consequences of various laws to universities, then stopped funding those universities, so the universities turned to corporations to fund them and the corporations paid for the results that they wanted on a truly epic scale, which then fed directly back into government making new law based on corporate-funded research. We broke the social machines that enabled moral decision-making at scale, and this is far from the only way those machines were compromised.

What is the damage done from all this erosion of accurate decision-making capacity? Well, is it carbohydrates, fats or salt that produce heart disease? Or is it job dissatisfaction? The answer depends very much on who you ask, but the fact that you cannot get a clear answer is a clear failure of the social machinery to deliver actionable truth to you, the individual decision-maker. A lot of people die over this question. Even worse, consider tobacco: *theoretically* smoking is a decision you are free to make, although tobacco consistently tops the charts on addictiveness and objective measures of harm from drugs, and somehow winds up available everywhere, all the time, as if it was as harmless as spring water. Is it really responsible to let people choose this? And, if so, why won't we let them have guns, hand grenades and various other things which would objectively kill far fewer people than the humble ciggie? You may say 'but guns kill other people' but so does secondary smoking. Government spends a lot of time telling people what to do and not to do. The resulting prohibitions and compulsions are badly irrational: homeless people cannot build homes, and it costs a billion dollars to get a new cancer drug to market.

So really we need trustworthy knowledge to make decisions, and especially to make law. We need people who are actually acting on our behalf, not on the behalf of their secret paymasters, to fight the power and tell us the truth that we need to know to make intelligent decisions on our own behalf. It's simply not fair to have enormous corporate interests corrupting our access to health information with bad science, advertising and illicit involvement with government regulators. Ordinary people cannot stand up to that kind of corrupting pressure, and when something goes wrong like the obesity epidemic we cannot get to the truth because nobody will fund the science, because what if it turns out to be something mundane, banal and wildly profitable, like the corn syrup industry or hormones in dairy products?

We are basically left defenceless against enormous machines which lie to us for a living, and we cannot blame people for hugging their crystals and waving spirulina and kale at this problem: after all, when you cannot access the truth through science, what could be more natural than turning to superstition? The scientific method works, but you have to apply it in a non-corrupt way to get trustworthy results.

And this is how we wound up in this mess: we can't get access to facts, and a huge machinery corrupts our sense of what is right for us personally. This is why our relationship with *stuff* has become so enormously toxic: toxic things made by a toxic machinery, detached from human welfare as an active consideration for the most part.

Our stuff is immoral, and *preys on our weakness with increasing intelligence*. This cannot go on.

AUTOMATED MORALITY IS THE ANSWER TO HUMAN WEAKNESS

When one writes a book about the future, eventually one has to resort to predictions. Here is mine.

In the future, we will be able to express our moral sentiments and other personal preferences to machines which will *provably act on our behalf and not on the behalf of others*, and those machines will intelligently do things such as prevent us being offered goods made by slave labour, or containing minerals from areas with active resource wars.

Those goods may still exist in the world, they may be for sale *somewhere*, but my prediction is that they will be automatically removed from sale, and stigmatised. To sell such goods to people under false pretences, in a way which disrupts their free choice to live by their own moral law, will be heavily penalised. An Amazon or an eBay could choose to discipline sellers, and provide a checkbox which says 'only show me things which are verified to be slavery-free' or 'only show me things which are vegan' quite easily at a technical level, but *the market itself usually cannot regulate the market.* It's going to take new social structures to control the force of capitalism, because government has tried and largely failed. That does not leave a permanent imbalance in which capital can do what it damn well likes forever: everything eventually finds its counterbalance, and this one is now overdue.

Stuff will continue to be made to conform to the profit motive: I am not suggesting a utopian future in which everybody works for free for the common weal, or where nobody works at all. But I am suggesting that, much as people keep kosher or are vegan, or keep Lent, people for the rest of foreseeable history will have personal ethical or moral codes which affect their purchasing patterns. People will rely on machines to make these decisions with them or for them because, in the future, nearly all of our other relationships with markets will be mediated by machines, so why shouldn't we also have machines to keep these markets moral? In the same way that nearly all airline tickets are booked using algorithms which systematically search through our options, sifting through the dazzling profusion of goods and services offered by capitalism and screening out the toxic dross is a job for algorithms: it is like email spam filtering for the physical world and the world of commerce.

This mechanism is the natural counterpart and controller for advertising. The dysfunctional role that stuff plays in our lives is a temporary phase, produced by the enormous imbalance between the powers of mass production combined with the cognitive science of targeted advertising, versus the meagre capabilities of individuals to take back control of their lives from these forces. But these tools are not inherently evil: rather, they can be turned to the good, and my prediction is that increasingly strident consumer objections to being lied to for decades in ways which killed millions of people (I'm looking at you, Big Tobacco) will eventually result in the creation of transparent and near-incorruptible technical and social machinery to answer simple questions we all want the answers to, like 'Is this poisoning me or anybody else?'

There is some progress towards this quest for objectivity. Services like DPReview and RTINGS do detailed scientific reports on the performance of certain classes of consumer electronics like cameras, monitors and headphones. They measure frequency responses and colour gamuts with laboratory equipment to give an objective basis for consumer decisions. This kind of objective truth cuts through advertising: a manufacturer can show me any shiny little film they like, but if I can get the specifications from an objective source, guess what I'm buying? I'm buying the one that works.

Correcting the balance of power between manufacturers, workers and buyers will take time. Scientific data about products alone is not enough to know whether a product is worthy of purchase: we must know about the social and environmental impacts of the product too. The imperative towards quality and accountability drives transparency, particularly in food or other products which may directly harm us. People will only allow themselves to be ruthlessly exploited by manufacturers for so long.

Just as the creation of the labour union to resist the overarching ambition of industrial-era employers was inevitable, algorithmic exploitation and secrecy about what we are buying must also have limits. We are in the early stages of creating new machinery to impose those limits.

Our stuff can and must become *kind*: if not actively life-giving, at least pleasant, friendly, and not hostile to its buyers or makers.

STUFF: BENIGN AND MALEVOLENT

Some of the things people try to sell you are going to kill you. Sometimes they know that, and obviously don't tell you. Sometimes they take active measures, for decades, to stop anybody figuring out how bad for you their products are. A lot of our *stuff* is mad defective. It is outrageous. Being sold this kind of *stuff* is as bad as the council planting the park with poison ivy and giant hogweed and then telling people to go out there for a nice picnic, failing to mention the poisonous weeds. Think I'm joking? Read about poisonous flame retardants in furniture. Or my old nemesis, the cigarette, who's theoretically less-toxic replacement, the e-cig, nearly killed a friend of mine. How do we wind up with cigarettes and toxic sofas and leaded petrol in cars and uninsulated houses poisoning our bodies and our atmosphere, all simultaneously destroying our futures? It is completely absurd – if an invading military force did this to us it would be a series of acts of war.

But somehow 'the market' can do this to us, and nobody seems to be invested in comprehensively stopping these ongoing atrocities and bringing the perpetrators to justice. It's like we're all fighting a war, every day, against other people secretly exploiting and harming us. How come all this bad stuff happens, and mysteriously it's no one's fault most of the time? Who's washing the hands here?

This problem is called *the agency problem*. People sell us things they know are bad for us because they get paid, we get screwed and the people who are paid to ask, 'Hey, is this stuff poisoning me or made by slave labour?' are remarkably ineffective. You just can't get these systems to work properly, because nobody's incentives in the system actually align with yours.

Countries create *agencies* to control the *agency* of the people who say they are here to help us, but mostly help themselves. In America, that's the Food and Drug Administration, or the Bureau of Alcohol, Tobacco and Firearms. Here in the UK it's the Food Standards Agency and the Department of Agriculture. But those agencies are only very weakly steered by the democratic mandate, because a vote at the ballot box turns into a change of direction at the FDA through a chain so long and so complex that a million votes together hardly steer it at all, while the employees of the agency spend every day talking to drug company spineless vipers who were hired specifically for their remarkable ability to hypnotise government officials back to sleep whenever they are woken up by some atrocity, and delay action on problematic situations as long as legally possible, and often much longer. The system is broken, and voting can't fix it, because the tie between the ballot box and the regulator is just too weak to get effective action. Representative democracy is the wrong level for fixing this problem, in the same way that you need both socialist governments *and* labour unions to get wages and working conditions fixed. The machinery has to be aligned.

As things stand today, past the food labelling and other statutory disclosures, you don't have a legal right to know what is in most of your products or how they were manufactured. The privacy and commercial secrecy rights of the people who make your *stuff* are treated as more important than your right to know *precisely what you are wearing on your skin or putting into your body*.

Even though I own it, even though I eat it, I still do not have the right to know *precisely* where this was grown, what (if any) pesticides were sprayed on it, or how it was processed and who processed it.

Nobody who keeps secrets like that from you is doing it for your welfare. They are exploiting you.

This pervasive exploitation and secrecy has become even more poisonous in the age of *smart stuff*. Amazon Alexa, Google Home, Apple Siri, Facebook and all the rest ship physical devices into your home (on request... they aren't built into new apartments as appliances... yet), which simply gather data, try to make you happy and build a more detailed profile about your mind than you, your mother, your therapist, your priest, or the government have. We certainly did not appoint these entities as Father Confessor over us, and yet, because it offers us useful services, we largely ignore the privacy downsides of *smart stuff*. It's there, it's pervasive, and increasingly it will be built into *everything*. And who watches these particular watchmen? Maybe the Federal Communications Commission, but consider our old friend tobacco again. Openly sold, and kills maybe half a million people each year in America alone. And that's fully regulated and heavily taxed. These systems are out of control.

What we have is a systemic problem: the means, the

motive and the opportunity exist to sell the general public *stuff* which is bad for them on nearly every imaginable axis, and only the most egregious assaults on the public weal run even the smallest risk of being brought to account. How on earth did we wind up here?

The answer is very simple: we bought ourselves into this mess, by accepting a profound lack of transparency and care from the companies we bring into existence by giving them our custom, and it's been this way for centuries, over a wide range of cultures. This is a pervasive problem.

Because we do not care to distinguish what is benign from what is malevolent in the marketplace with sufficient discrimination, and do not force the issue by boycott when the truth is not forthcoming, corporate bad actors repeatedly abuse the public trust and face no consequences of note. We lack the *social machinery* to detect this kind of pervasive abuse and put a stop to it, in much the same way that until the invention of the labour union and universal suffrage we lacked the machinery to rein in abusive employers and our feudal overlords. We have left the job of watching the chicken coop to a variety of foxes, some corporate, some state, and all entirely too comfortable with the status quo around product safety and your right to make decisions about your life based on accurate information. This is not an equilibrium which will stand much longer. Let me explain why.

Firstly, the systems which could effectively protect us from fraud and exploitation are the same systems that could build new classes of economic efficiency. Simply by knowing what things are in a very detailed way, we can make efficient use of them, perhaps in ways their creators did not even intend. And what's more, these systems based on deep transparency will help companies to sell their products. If there is a machine-readable exact specification of what something is, I can send software out to search for the things I need. In an industrial context, this model is potentially all-powerful: fully automated procurement, supply chain and logistics.

As ordinary shoppers, we would get clothes that always fit, because of a perfect match between our bodies and the clothes, and both can be measured with a tape measure. It's not hard to gather the data, we just lack the *machinery* to do it. It is absurd that the fashion industry does not already work this way. When things reach the end of their usefulness, if machines know what a thing is, it can be efficiently resold or recycled without further human inconvenience. All these economic benefits will only accrue to companies that are transparent about what they are offering the world, and that economic pressure is one of our best allies in the fight for control of our lives through control of our stuff.

Product safety and automated product discoverability are aspects of the same process: product transparency. That transparency also gives us the necessary keys for automated morality: our software can act on our ethical instructions, not just our commercial ones.

But this kind of deep transparency about products will also reveal to us the actual living and working conditions of the people who make our stuff. If, for your own safety, you want to know where your stuff comes from, you are going to be stuck with a lot of disturbing knowledge about sweatshops and primary resource extraction like mining. You are not going to want to know a lot of these additional answers in many cases. The price of prosperity is all too often ecocide and oppression. The fun consumer product in front of you was, all too often, manufactured from toxic plastics in dangerous ways by people who lacked workplace safety or labour protections. But the process that will let you know *just how dangerous* those plastics are will *necessarily* involve transparency about the rest of the process.

You may say, 'How could anybody do business in such a world?' to which my reply is simply, 'How could anybody expect to survive in this one?'

Because the mother of all pollutants is carbon dioxide. And you do not know, when you buy something, how much harm you are doing yourself, the planet and the future of life on earth. *This is simply unacceptable.* We have to know how much carbon was emitted to make things. We can't get the change necessary to fix global warming (and all the rest) unless we can assess who is doing the damage and stop them. As of 2020, this is a matter of *some urgency*.

Global warming not only threatens our way of life, it threatens life's way of life.

Sudden change rips species' ecological niches right out from under them and leaves them hurtling into freefall towards an unforgiving ground. In objective terms, it is vastly more important to the future of the world that governments and individuals can track their carbon emissions than that everybody can track their money, and yet none of the machinery exists to build pervasive control of our carbon economy, and stop carbon overspending before it destroys our ecological balance. Yet corporations still track their money down to the cent. Something is wrong.

The same situation repeats and overlaps in areas like deforestation and emission of hormone-mimicking chemicals into the environment and into our bodies. All the way through, we have lost control of these processes because the industrial revolution and globalisation massively ramped up the complexity of the world in ways that made it very difficult for us to actually know *what was really happening to us*. Weird chemicals, defective industrial processes, hugely complex systemic problems like CO_2 all skip neatly around our biological and cultural systems about how to identify and deal with threats, and we are taking an absolute pounding from bad actors who live in our blind spots.

Regulators can't regulate, customers can't get the information they need to make decisions and the disaster continues. During the COVID crisis in early 2020 fake masks were aggressively injected into the medical supply chain by unscrupulous fraudsters, possibly costing many lives, particularly among medical staff.

We have not built an immune system to deal with the future, with the fallout from industrialisation, and we are not going forwards without building one. We must be able to separate the *benign* from the *malevolent* in everything we touch. This has to happen in an automated, reliable way which allows us to live our lives, and not get constantly exposed to other people's poisons or the general consequences of industrial carelessness or deliberate exploitation. Is it bad for me? For society? For biology? For the future? For the world? I need to know.

We must know, so that we can be free.

THE FUTURE OF STUFF

We have no idea what technology will bring us in future. Fifty years from now, most *stuff* will probably be made of materials we could not identify in a lab if we were handed them today, built using manufacturing techniques we cannot even guess at. I make that claim based on a simple fact: change is accelerating. Every year since the start of the Second World War things have changed imperceptibly faster than they changed before, until the change is so fast it becomes a blur. I tell people these days – and mostly believe – that my expected lifespan is 400 years because at forty-eight in 2020 there's every chance of really significant breakthroughs in life-extension technology before I die, and once you get on the life-extension train, every year that passes extends your life by more than one more year because of scientific progress.

I make an arbitrary limit at 400 because that's what they do in the Culture, Iain M. Banks's anarchist sci-fi utopia. They sort of fade out as they get older, and at a certain point I expect to do much the same. But not yet. Not for centuries. *Centuries.*

The stuff, against that lifespan, is as ephemeral as a breeze. Books rot, electronics become first obsolete and then get reclassified as toxic waste because of all the lead and cadmium in them. Buildings get replaced because they are so energy inefficient, replaced with spun glass or genetically engineered timber which grows straight and square and obeys the architect, right from the seed.

Is this unrealistic?

Not at all. My first computer was a ZX81 bought in 1982. I've watched its cousins turn into gigantic, almost cosmic, world-spanning machines, reaching out into space, and here and there, deep space, a single, interconnected digital substrate for consciousness filled with people trading cat GIFs and insulting each other's mothers over their political beliefs. Forty years seems like a long time, but against a 400-year

VINAY GUPTA

lifespan it's the blink of an eye. And if I'm not around to see all of this, somebody much like me will be! The stuff goes by in the blink of an eye.

Even if my *natural* 400-year span is foreshortened to only another twenty years, in those twenty years I expect to see humanoid robots doing most cleaning and many service industry jobs, and artificial intelligence perfected to the point where real-time machine translation of speech and video is possible, so it looks as if all TV shows and movies were made in all languages.

I expect to be able to say, 'Okay, play me "Waterloo" by ABBA as if it had been sung by Björk around the time of *Debut* and have a barely perceptible pause as computers figure out the details for me and play me an impossible song. It's quite good, but not as good as Nick Cave and Trent Reznor's version of 'Baby, It's Cold Outside'.

But even in this world to come I expect nearly all the existing nation states still to exist, and most of today's tech giants to still be significant forces for quite some decades. Some will implode, new ones will be created and computers will be yesterday's 'new hotness' as the genetic engineers seriously get to work producing the *stuff* we have always wanted but never knew we could have: houseplants that clean the air and just won't die; buildings made by growing trees; new organs – not just replacements for what we *have already* but *new organs* that do *new things*; and maybe, even, possibly,

58

finally, cats with the friendly temperament of dogs. But the enormous innovation capacity of the big computer technology companies will not stay digital: they'll go biotech as soon as it is profitable, so many of these biotech wonders will come from players we recognise today, by acquisition and transformation. These companies are the new nations, right beside the existing ones. Nations whose borders are defined by patents not landmarks, and who tax by price rises, rather than by income, but mighty nations nonetheless.

Time is going to whizz by us in an almost imperceptible, incomprehensible blur. Just think about phones: hand-cranked devices where operators dialled the numbers for you, then rotary dial slabs of plastic and metal tethered to the wall by a wire, then mobiles the size of remote controls, then the first early linking of phones and the Internet over WAP, then generation after generation of smartphones. What wonder will be called 'a phone' in twenty years?

And yet... 'phone' will likely remain, as primitive a concept as 'hammer'. Whatever else it does, the thing I used to talk to my friends about is *the phone* regardless of what else it does.

What is enduring about *stuff* is not stuff, it's *people*. In describing the social architecture that produces our *stuff* and describing the great cultural, political and social struggles that define our manufacturing economy, I want to frame a single concept clearly in your minds: *patterns are produced by processes*. Stuff is made by processes, and not just chemical or industrial processes; cultural, financial, political and social processes all combine to produce this stuff we see before us. It has patterns because it comes from processes.

When you can see the enduring, durable social structures which go into producing your stuff, you will no longer be distracted and amazed by the glossy, glitzy wonderland of the *stuff* in the malls and the web stores. You'll be able to stop and ask the hard questions: *what is in this stuff*? Who made this stuff? Is this stuff wrecking the world? What does this stuff really do for me? What does this stuff really do *to* me? And you'll be sensitised to the fresh green shoots as we start, as a culture, to turn against *malevolent stuff* that poisons us and our world, strips us of our rights and crushes people in its production. Together, we can build the social and cultural immune systems which will expand the rights of consumers, year by year, generation by generation, to know *exactly* what decision they are making when they decide to buy a product, because they know *exactly* what the product is and where the product came from. Consumers, empowered in this way, can completely transform how the economy works. No more accidentally buying the wrong things and having to return them. No more nasty surprises when you plug A into B and it just doesn't work. No more buying things just as they become obsolete. It can all go away, and inevitably it will.

Getting right to the heart of the matter, this is about power. Right now, the people who sell us our stuff wield the power of secrecy over us, and we let them. Stripping back that veil will often be a painful process, but the leaders in that transformation will be both heroes and the most successful entrepreneurs of the future. Because, unlike voters, consumers do not have to interface with centuries of codified law to change the rules of the game they live inside of: they can just buy *different, better stuff* and effect transformation immediately.

I want to know what is in the products I buy every day. Are you with me?

QUALITY AND QUALIA

> 'What's wrong with technology is that it is not con-
> nected to any real way with matters of the spirit and
> the heart. And so it does blind, ugly things quite by
> accident and gets hated for that. People haven't paid
> much attention to this before because the big concern
> has been for food, clothing and shelter for everyone
> and technology has provided these'
>
> – Robert M. Pirsig, *Zen and the*
> *Art of Motorcycle Maintenance*

I am an engineer, and I am unsentimental about *stuff*. My emotional attachments to art, other than music, are shallow. I own perhaps one sculpture, and no paintings. No photos, no memorabilia. I could perhaps equip a small expeditionary party from my garage, but you won't find a loom or a display case in my home. As a man interested in function, I view stuff through a specific lens: I can identify which kind of USB cable you hold in your hand from across a room, and I probably have a matching one in my bag.

So this story that I have told you about *stuff* is an engineer's journey into the heart of why the things we buy are often of such low quality, and a direct product of my work on trying to make better things over decades. My biggest contribution to the world of stuff is my refugee shelter design, the hexayurt, which has been open source for most of twenty years and is built by the thousand by ordinary festival-goers, and one or two disaster relief companies. A cruder and more functional building you could not hope to see. I have proofs!

But occasionally I visit my friend Robert Brewer Young, a luthier, who is often to be found with a Stradivarius violin in his intelligent hands. The violin is, by any reasonable metric, a sacred object if only because of the centuries of worship that have surrounded it. And, yes, at one point in its history, right back at the start, it came from a sort of factory and was sold as a tool.

Now it is surrounded by a halo, and then bow is put to string, and *something happens*.

Do not forget there is stuff in this world that is a vehicle for the expression of the human soul.

AFTERWORD

In 1924, inspired by a sensational essay they had published the previous year, the publishers Kegan Paul launched a series of small, elegant books called To-Day and To-Morrow. The founding essay was *Daedalus; or, Science and the Future*, and its author, the biologist J. B. S. Haldane, made several striking predictions: genetic modification, wind power, artificial food. But the idea that captured the imagination of his contemporaries was what he called 'ectogenesis' – the gestation of embryos in artificial wombs. Haldane's friend Aldous Huxley included it in his novel *Brave New World*, in which humans are cloned and mass-produced in 'Hatcheries' (it was Haldane who later gave us the word 'clone'). Fast-forward almost a century, and scientists have now trialled ectogenesis on sheep and are exploring its potential for saving dangerously premature babies.

Haldane took no prisoners as he hurtled through the ages and all the major sciences, weighing up what was still to be done. Perhaps because it was his discipline, he was convinced that the next exciting scientific discoveries would be made not in physics but in biology. So, his Daedalus is not the familiar pioneer of flight but the first genetic engineer – the designer of the contraption that enabled King Minos's wife to mate with a bull and produce the Minotaur. Predictions have an unstable afterlife; their truth changes with the world, and while Haldane was brilliant on – and made a major contribution to – genetics, he was sceptical about the possibility of nuclear power. In the wake of the Second World War, and the realities of atom bombs, hydrogen bombs and nuclear power stations, his view of the sciences appeared wide of the mark. Later, when the Human Genome Project became news, he emerged as a prophet again. But while biotech certainly still preoccupies us two decades on, it is the computer that we see ushering in the definitive transformations of the age: artificial intelligence, machine learning, blockchain. And, remarkably, the computer is the one major modern development that not only Haldane but all the To-Day and To-Morrow writers missed.

By 1931, when the series was wound up, it ran to 110 books. They covered many of the subjects that mattered most at the time, from the future of marriage to the future of war, the future of art to the future of the British Empire. Most of To-Day and To-morrow's contributors were progressive, rationalist and intelligent, in favour of a World State and sceptical of eugenics. They wrote well, and were sometimes very funny, and the essays on the future of clothes and the future of nonsense in particular are wonderfully eccentric. And, of course, Haldane wasn't the only visionary. Many of the other writers contributed equally far-sighted ideas: Dora Russell suggested something akin to universal basic income for mothers; J. D. Bernal imagined wirelessly networked cyborgs – a cross between social media and the Internet of things; while Vera Brittain waxed confident about the enshrinement of women's rights in law.

What really stands out now is how, on the whole, the authors seemed to feel freer to be imaginative about the future than our contemporaries tend to be when they make predictions. There seems to be something about the long-form essay that freed the To-Day and To-morrow authors to see further ahead than a short journalistic piece could. Pursuing the logic of an individual vision, while also responding to what others projected, led them to dive deep into their topics in ways that are hard for the more tightly collaborative think-tank approaches of today to replicate. They were also more constructive than most of our contemporary future-thinkers. Of course we'd be mad not to worry about the climate crisis, the mass displacement of people(s), the risks of AI, new diseases (I'm writing this at the height – *maybe* – of COVID-19), asteroid collision and other apocalyptic scenarios. But if we're not only to survive these but also to thrive, we need to think beyond them as well as about them.

We are now almost a century on from the launch of To-Day and Tomorrow, and it feels like the right time to try this thought experiment again. So, for this first set of FUTURES, we have assembled a diverse group of brilliant writers with provocative ideas and visions. The point is not so much to prophesy as to generate new ideas about possibilities that could help us realise a future we might want to inhabit. To-Day and To-Morrow launched visions that helped create the modern world. The challenges we face now are, obviously, different from those of the 1920s and 30s. But our aspirations for FUTURES are the same. We want to change the conversation about what lies ahead so we can better imagine, understand and articulate the new worlds we might want to create.

Professor Max Saunders, March 2020

Max Saunders's Imagined Futures: Writing, Science, and Modernity in the To-Day and To-Morrow Book Series, 1923–31 *was published by Oxford University Press in 2019.*

Unbound is the world's first crowdfunding publisher, established in 2011.

We believe that wonderful things can happen when you clear a path for people who share a passion. That's why we've built a platform that brings together readers and authors to crowdfund books they believe in – and give fresh ideas that don't fit the traditional mould the chance they deserve.

This book is in your hands because readers made it possible. Everyone who pledged their support is listed below. Join them by visiting unbound.com and supporting a book today.

With special thanks to Jo Greenslade and Ark Schools

Caspar Addyman
Kathy Allen
John Attridge
William Ayles
Stuart Banks
David Barker
Stephen Beagrie
Ghassan Bejjani
Sarah Bennett
James Benussi

Steve Bindley
Kate Bird
Ian Blatchford
Su Bonfanti
Ed Bonnell
Stuart Bowdler
John Boxall
Zara Bredin
Catherine Breslin
Fabia Bromovsky

Victoria Bryant
Nicki Burns
Paul David Burns
Imogen Butler
Steve Byrne
Bob Callard
Ella Cape-Davenhill
NJ Cesar
Neil Chavner
Brendan Clarke

Nick Clarke

Peter Clasen

Jane Clifford

Fiona Clifft

Rhonda Cole

David-John Collins

Robert Collins

Alexander Colmer

Laura Colombino

Joseph Cordery

Andrew Correia

Peter Cosgrove

Nicola Crowell

Paolo Cuomo

Mary Curnock
    Cook

Matthew d'Ancona

Tom Daly

Eileen Davidson

Joshua Davies

Edmund Davison

Victoria Davison

Sarah Denton

Jeremy Dicker

Lewis Dimmick

Kevin Donnellon

Linda Edge

Helen Edwards

Michael Elliott

Dominic Emery

Nic Fallows

Joanna Flood

Graham Folmer

Cedric Fontanille

Robert Forsyth

Oliver Francis

D Franklin

The FUTURES
    team

Josh Gaillemin

Brian Gee

Lisa Gee

Sarah Gee

Charley Gilbert

Tom Gillingwater

Jordan Goble

George Goodfellow

John Gordon

Molly Gordon

Paul Gould

Brice Goureau

Melanie Gow

Keith Grady

Marlies Gration

Jon Gray

Scott Greenwell

Georgia Greer

John Grout

Steve Grycuk

Nicola Haggett

Greg Halfacre

Elizabeth Hall

Skye Hallam

Chloe Hardy

Nicola Harford

Richard Harvey

Nick Helweg-
    Larsen

Paul Higgins

Gemma Hitchens

Maggie Hobbs

Meaghan Hook

Simon Howard

Nick Hubble

Simon Huggins

Jenny Hynd

Maggie Jack

Andy Johnson

Rebecca Jones

Danny Josephs

Tanu Kaskinen

Matthew Keegan

Christopher Kelly

Hilary Kemp

Luke Kemp

Fraser Kerr

Adam Khan

Dan Kieran

Andrew Knight

Christine Knight-
 Maunder

Lauren Knussen

Florian Kogler

Michael Kowalski

Simon Krystman

Nikki Land

Ben Lappin

Lyndsey Lawrence

Benedict Leigh

Fiona Lensvelt

Max Lensvelt

Sonny Leong

Miriam Levitin

Joanne Limburg

Linds

Valerie Lindsay

Ivan Lowe

Brian Lunn

Nicola Lynch

Rob MacAndrew

Andrew MacGarvey

Jem Mackay

Innes Macleod

Lewis MacRae

Paul Martin

Chris Matthias

Jenny McCullough

Michael McDowall

John McGowan

Neil McLaren

Adrian Melrose

John Mitchinson

Ronald Mitchinson

Kyna Morgan

Ian Morley

Tony Mulvahil

Robin Mulvihill

Peter Mummery

Tessa Murray

Janet Musgrove

James Nash

Carlo Navato

Kelvin Nel

John New

Sorcha Ní
 Mhaonaigh

Christopher Norris

Tim O'Connor

Mark O'Neill

Brian Padley

Michael Paley

Euan Palmer

Nic Parsons

Jaynesh Patel

Don Paterson

Sumit Paul-
 Choudhury

Matthew Pearson

Pauline Peirce

Nick Petre

Benjamin Poliak

Justin Pollard

Harriet Posner

Samantha Potter

Mark Poulson

Kate Pullinger

Slam Raman

Padraig Reade

Colette Reap

Suzanne Reynolds

John Rice Doyle

Stephen Ross

Charlotte Rump

Stuart Rutherford

Keith Ruttle

Cassedy Ryan

Ruth Sacks

Luke Sanders

Martin Saugnac
Max Saunders
Eleanor Scharer
Daniel Schwickerath
Duncan Scovil
Alexander Sehmer
Rossa Shanks
Gillian Shearn
Paul Skinner
Christopher Smith
Jan Smith
Katie Smith
Matthew Spicer
Paul Squires
Wendy Staden
Nicola Stanhope

Keith Stewart
Freddie Stockler
Nick Stringer
Elizabeth Suffling
Gilane Tawadros
Georgette Taylor
Richard Taylor
Bronwen Thomas
Luke Thornton
Lydia Titterington
Sophie Truepenny
Mark Turner
Geoff Underwood
Maarten van den
    Belt
Suzan Vanneck

Danielle Vides
Emma Visick
Gabriel Vogt
Claire Walker
Sir Harold Walker
Suzi Watford
Richard White
John Williams
Ross Williams
Catherine
    Williamson
Philip Wilson
Luke Young
Angelique &
    Stefano Zuppet